New Orleans Mardi Gras Moments

Judi Bottoni and Peggy Scott Laborde

PELICAN PUBLISHING COMPANY

Gretna 2015

The word "Pelican" and the depiction of a pelican are trademarks of Pelican Publishing Company, Inc., and are registered in the U.S. Patent and Trademark Office.

ISBN: 9781455621194
E-book ISBN: 9781455621200

Printed in China

Published by Pelican Publishing Company, Inc.
1000 Burmaster Street, Gretna, Louisiana 70053

Contents

Introduction by Judi Bottoni

Upon first moving to New Orleans, I could not help but recognize the visual and cultural feast that the city serves up on a daily basis. It is understandable why this famous crescent in a bend of the mighty Mississippi became a magnet for artists and writers the likes of Edgar Degas and Tennessee Williams and why this humble transplanted photographer from upstate New York was immediately captivated by its sights, sounds, smells, tastes, and emotions. What it is that draws the artist in all of us to this special place has been debated for years. Perhaps it is our makeup—a cultural gumbo with everything thrown into the pot. Or maybe it is the ever-present humidity cloaking the city in dreamy hues, dampening edges, and spurring the imagination to see beyond the obvious. All I know is that once I arrived here, I never left.

Carnival is a photographer's delight! It is time of dazzling colors, dancing lights, excited energy, and ever so much more. From float riders throwing out their shiny beads to flambeaux carriers twirling blazing torches, the visual senses are inflamed. Make no mistake about it— Mardi Gras is "art" in and of itself. The living canvas can be quite large and unwieldy and sometimes that is the effect I want, but I can also pick and choose from its details for a more immediate focus. It is important to go beyond the surface colors and lights and dig deeper into moods and emotions. With each photograph I must ask, "What makes this scene or image different from the one down the block, or the one I caught last year, or even that exposed by hundreds of other photographers drawn to the same spot?" Photography is so much more than a mere snapshot or a quick push on a smart-phone screen. It must tell a story. This is where artistry and poetry literally enter the picture.

My thanks to all who have stood by me in this project, sitting with me through endless parades and pageantries while I waited for the perfect shot, helping carry ladders and equipment to let me focus on my work, and giving me new perspectives on my photographs as I molded them into a comprehensive work. Without these professionals and countless friends, my goals for this publication could not have been reached. My special thanks to Lisa Slatten. Also, special thanks to the memory of my parents, Theresa and Peter Bottoni; to my uncle, Paris Bottoni, for his support; and to my cousins Francis and Barbara Valone.

Finally I give my sincerest thanks to the readers of this book for allowing me the opportunity to briefly spark their imaginations and share a celebration that is very dear to my heart. While my goal has been to capture Mardi Gras through the tools of photography, in truth, it is Mardi Gras itself that has captured me. Hopefully all who see my images will have as much fun in the viewing as I have had in the making of them.

Introduction by Peggy Scott Laborde

My earliest memories of Mardi Gras consist of dressing up as a cowgirl, complete with fringed hat. My parents took me and my brother and sister downtown to see the Rex parade near the corner of Canal Street and St. Charles. In the late 1950s we caught beads made of glass from Czechoslovakia and strands of colored rice wrapped in wax paper. By 1960 Rex maskers began throwing doubloons, the aluminum coins that have become a Carnival staple.

Sometimes on Mardi Gras Day we would also get a chance to see King Zulu early in the morning and even some truck parades later in the day. During the week before, we just might see a nighttime parade on St. Charles Avenue.

My, how things have changed. The New Orleans Carnival has exploded: more parades, more varieties of throws. And while it is still *our* celebration, it has become part of the city's economic lifeblood.

Today's Carnival season includes multi-parade nights on the St. Charles Avenue route, cleverly costumed sub-krewes that often march within larger parades, and some smaller satirical processions that remind us we can still poke fun at ourselves. Right now there are fifty-three parades! This number includes those that are within Orleans Parish and in the suburbs.

In **New Orleans Mardi Gras Moments**, photographer Judi Bottoni and I will show you today's celebration—maskers, floats, and more. We will share glimpses of some of the well-known celebrities who have participated and the lesser-known aspects of the season that can be equally fascinating. It would be totally impossible to include every moment of Mardi Gras. It all depends on where you are standing, whether it be on St. Charles Avenue, Canal Street, Bourbon Street, or North Claiborne Avenue.

Just as each and every strand of beads that I caught as

While masking may date back to ancient times, it's alive and well in New Orleans during Carnival.

In addition to clown costumes, many young New Orleans Mardi Gras revelers dressed up as cowboys and cowgirls during the 1950s. Center is coauthor Peggy Scott Laborde, with brother, Kurt, sister, Nancy, and father, Warren James Scott.

a child was precious, so are the new memories of a celebration where color, creativity, and pure joy can make for endless possibilities.

In the following pages, we provide our own "show and tell." Photographer Judi Bottoni chronicles scenes from what is easily the world's largest celebration of Carnival. I have the pleasure of sharing with you some backstories on the New Orleans Mardi Gras and what is involved in staging pageantry on such a lavish scale.

Finally, before we proceed, for a more in-depth history of the New Orleans Carnival let me recommend historian and *New Orleans Magazine* editor-in-chief Errol Laborde's book, ***Mardi Gras: Chronicles of the New Orleans Carnival,*** also published by Pelican. (Yes, we are related—Errol is my spouse.)

Special thanks to Errol for his continued support of all of my projects. His wisdom and expertise is invaluable. Also thanks to my late parents, Gloria and Warren Scott, sister, Nancy, and brother, Kurt, for sharing early Mardi Gras adventures. And to the memory of my aunt and uncle June and Irving Scott for their passion for Mardi Gras.

As always, I am grateful to my friends Beth Arroyo Utterback, executive vice-president/chief operating officer of WYES-TV, and Dominic Massa, executive producer for WWL-TV, for their encouragement and good cheer. Judi Bottoni and I also want to acknowledge Arthur Hardy, publisher of *Arthur Hardy's Mardi Gras Guide*. Over the years Judi has photographed the annual celebration for Arthur, and I am grateful for his willingness to share information.

I want to thank my friends Doris Ann Gorman, who has always been so very helpful with her vast research skills, and Jules Richard IV, ready to assist during the Carnival season whenever needed. And finally, a big shout out to Pelican Publishing Company. Kathleen Calhoun Nettleton's confidence in this book means so very much. And of course much appreciation to Nina Kooij, Erin Classen, Antoinette de Alteriis, Jefferey Hench, and designer Cassie Zimmerman for making ***New Orleans Mardi Gras Moments*** as beautiful as they are in real life.

Royal Street is a favorite route for some of the smaller marching clubs that traverse the French Quarter on Mardi Gras Day.

New Orleans Mardi Gras Moments

The riding lieutenants of the Rex organization wear purple, gold, and green costumes. Note Rex in the background on the float made especially for His Highness.

Chapter One
"Throw Me Some Info, Mister!"

We have the Romans to thank. The ancient festival of Lupercalia consisted of raucous behavior, lots of wine, and a general good time. Held in mid-February, the celebration was staged to ward off evil spirits. Rituals to ensure fertility and an easy childbirth consisted of men scantily clad in goatskins running down the road using strips of animal skins to gently lash ladies who were lined up.

Becoming tamer through the years, the annual event was transformed by Christianity into Carnivale, the tradition of feasting before the fasting of the forty days of Lent. The Fatted Calf, or Boeuf Gras, has become the symbol of "Farewell to the Flesh." Predominantly Catholic France observed this date from the country's earliest days.

In New Orleans, founded in 1718, Mardi Gras traditions carried forth from the mother country, allowing for a day of revelry even in this tiny, often mud-filled colony. Miscellaneous maskers poured out into the streets on Mardi Gras and packed the numerous ballrooms in the evening.

While in the 1830s an attempt was made to establish a cohesive procession of maskers on Mardi Gras Day itself, it wasn't until 1857 that the first organized parade took place. It created a template for what followed. A group of local businessmen, many from the East Coast, formed Comus, named after a Greek god known for his revelry and mischievous behavior. The colorful torch-lit procession consisted of walking figures made of papier-mâché and some members on horseback. Held on the night of Mardi Gras, Comus staged a ball after its procession in a downtown theater.

The popularity of Comus inspired other organizations during the nineteenth century, including the Twelfth Night Revelers, Momus, and Proteus. But 1872 would see the dawning of the first organized daytime parade, albeit rag-tag the first time out.

Rex, King of Carnival, was created by some local businessmen and a newspaper editor who wanted to send a message to the rest of the United States that New Orleans was open for business despite the challenges of Reconstruction. The visit of a Russian grand duke, Alexis Romanov, coincided with Mardi Gras that year, adding a certain amount of luster that was perfect for publicity.

The founders of Rex made several proclamations in the local newspapers leading up to the royal arrival on February 13, 1872. These included the suggestion that citizens decorate their balconies with banners using the colors purple, gold, and green, chosen based on the rules of heraldry. Of the allowed heraldry colors, red, white, and blue had already flown in the United States and Europe as the colors of revolution. But Rex was a monarch: purple, gold, and green are very fit for a king, if only for a day.

These nascent parades often touted a theme that was based in classic mythology or literature. The organizations, called "krewes" (an Old English spin on the word "crews" confected by members of Comus), used the employees of the revered French Opera House and other theatres for the construction of floats and backdrops for masked balls.

The celebration of a Carnival season officially kicked off with the observance of Twelfth Night (January 6) with balls and the consumption of a pastry known as king cake. In honor of the visit of the Three Kings to the Christ Child,

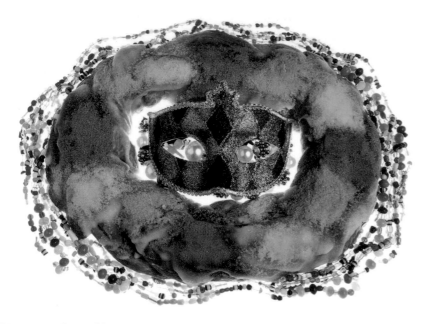

Eating a slice of king cake on Twelfth Night is a New Orleans Carnival tradition. With medieval roots, the cake was baked in celebration of the visit of the Three Kings to the Christ Child. Today a plastic baby is included inside, representing Jesus. Tradition is that whoever gets the baby in their slice is supposed to buy the next king cake or hold the next party.

a porcelain baby representing the Christ Child was contained within the pastry. Another variation of the king cake hails from France. Sometimes instead of a representation of the Christ Child, a mere bean was hidden inside the cake. Today, a plastic baby is the most common trinket in king cakes in New Orleans.

In 1909, the Zulu Social Aid and Pleasure Club debuted. This walking club, with an initially informal serpentine route, has grown into a full-sized parade on Mardi Gras. Painted coconuts are favorite souvenirs.

While there had already been many Carnival balls during the 1930s, some local businessmen expanded the season with the creation of the Babylon, Carrollton, and Hermes parades. Other groups followed, though none paraded during World War II and the Korean War.

Since the late '50s, more than sixteen all-female parades have come and gone in the area. Still parading from that time is Iris, which debuted in 1959.

By the 1960s, there was a general feeling that the annual Mardi Gras celebration had become tired and that expansion might attract more visitors. In 1969 Bacchus became the first "super-krewe" and instead of a local king chose a nationally known celebrity as its monarch. The creation of a busy parade schedule the weekend before Mardi Gras Day itself became a tourist draw.

Endymion, which began in the late 1960s as a neighborhood parade, evolved into a super-krewe that is now the longest parade in the New Orleans Carnival; it fills the Saturday evening slot.

1979 was a challenging year for Mardi Gras. Union members of the New Orleans Police Department went on strike right before the beginning of the parade season. Supporting Mayor Ernest "Dutch" Morial, most of the krewes cancelled their parades, with a few relocating to the suburbs. The strike fell apart. On Mardi Gras Day, many revelers still filled the French Quarter for what turned out to be a pleasant, peaceful day. To fill in for striking officers, National Guard unit soldiers were assigned to give protection. Maskers stood next to soldiers to have their photo taken, proof positive that the celebration continued regardless.

In 1987 Rex once again began arriving at the foot of Canal Street by ship on the day before Mardi Gras, a tradition that had taken place until 1917. Now featuring some added pomp and circumstance, including fireworks, today that Monday is known as "Lundi Gras."

Council Member-At-Large Dorothy Mae Taylor introduced an ordinance in 1991 calling for the integration of Mardi Gras krewes. According to Carnival historian Errol Laborde, the "complex social issues had less to do with race and more to do with traditions and the government's role in regulating freedom of association." The ultimate fallout was that Comus stopped parading. Momus and Proteus also vanished from the streets, with the latter returning in 2000 and the former eventually returning with a new name, Chaos.

The 1990s witnessed a parade boom starting with the satirical Le Krewe d'Etat. Orpheus, another super-krewe with echoes of nine-teenth-century classical float design, began in 1994; and a new all-female krewe named Muses debuted in 2001, throwing clever trinkets and filled with a myriad of clever walking clubs. A highlight of the era's krewe creation is the Krewe of the Rolling Elvi, a group that dresses as Elvis Presley and rides motor scooters.

Ancient Druids debuted in 1999, Pygmalion the next year. Knights of Chaos, another clever satirical procession, took to the streets in 2001, with Excalibur and Morpheus joining the ranks in 2002.

2006 was a year that exacted many challenges to Carnival. In the throes of 2005's Hurricane Katrina and recovery, there was controversy as to whether the city should stage parades during such difficult times, especially for the poor. Groups including Zulu felt strongly that the message to the rest of the world should be that New Orleans was open for business.

In 2012 another female krewe, Nyx, arrived on the

Krewe of Zulu warriors walk the parade route on Mardi Gras Day.

scene. Muses' signature throw is a decorated shoe; Nyx disseminates decorated purses.

With so many members having suffered from AIDS during the 1970s and '80s, gay Carnival ball organizations are now experiencing a resurgence. Satyricon and Amon-Ra are among the senior groups that work hard every year to create lavish costumes for their tableaus.

Today, there are Mardi Gras organizations both large and small. To illustrate the small side, the 'tit Rəx group consists of a procession of decorated floats made from shoeboxes! The Intergalactic Krewe of Chewbacchus pays homage to characters from the *Star Wars* franchise and sci-fi and fantasy films in general.

As popular as throws become in all shapes and forms, there's a small but growing movement to create trinkets by hand and to use recycled products.

One thing that hasn't changed over the years is the ability of New Orleanians to enjoy the season, regardless of what's in our pocketbooks. Parade krewe members throw beads and miscellaneous items to crowds at their own expense. That generosity is part of what makes the New Orleans Carnival so endearing.

Actor Will Ferrell, who has made many movies in New Orleans, served as Bacchus in 2012.

The all-female Krewe of Muses is known for handing out decorated shoes to the crowd.

Chapter Two

Kicking Off the Carnival Season

Twelfth Night, January 6, is the day when king cakes go on sale all over town, even though there are sightings beforehand. In the Christian calendar this is the day the Three Kings visited the Christ Child. The oblong ring-shaped cake, more resembling a brioche, contained a bean or trinket called a feve, often resembling a baby, representing the Christ Child.

Traditionally, whoever found a feve in their slice of the dessert was to give the next party or, in more recent times, purchase the next king cake.

By the 1930s the New Orleans-based McKenzie's bakeries began producing the confection in mass quantities and promoting them through mass marketing. Over the years, other bakeries have overshadowed McKenzie's coffee cake-style confection, creating cream-filled concoctions in a rainbow of flavors. And now, thanks to FedEx, UPS, and other package carriers, you can send a New Orleans-style king cake just about anywhere in the world.

In 1870, the Twelfth Night Revelers began staging balls for their members and even paraded for a few years. During the ball a court of young ladies are handed tiny boxes from within a giant replica of a cake. Whoever receives the box with a gold-colored bean is proclaimed queen.

Now, over a century later, there's a public pronouncement of the carnival season's kickoff by a group called the Phunny Phorty Phellows.

Deriving their name from a satirical organization that paraded in New Orleans from 1878 to 1898, the Phunny Phorty Phellows are also known as the PPP. In 1981 the group marched in the Krewe of Clones. Organized under the auspices of the then-new Contemporary Arts Center, many small sub-krewes banded together

The Twelfth Night Revelers, a New Orleans Carnival organization that started in 1870, stages their ball on January 6. Before the ball begins, krewe members parade through part of the French Quarter and dine at a local restaurant.

The Phunny Phorty Phellows announce the beginning of the Carnival season with their annual streetcar ride on Twelfth Night, January 6.

Before their annual streetcar ride, the Phunny Phorty Phellows receive a toast from the Krewe of Oak.

under the Clones' "umbrella" to march around the French Quarter and the Central Business District a few weeks before Carnival. They all loosely followed a satirical theme. Once the Clones stopped parading in the mid-'80s, most of the krewes united under the name Krewe du Vieux.

But not so the Phunny Phorty Phellows. In 1982, inspired by a member who had a birthday party aboard a St. Charles Avenue streetcar, the group decided to have their own procession via streetcar on the evening of January 6.

Calling themselves the "heralds" of Carnival, the Phellows' (the term covering both genders) costumed and masked members arrive and greet what has now grown

to be a large crowd of well-wishers at the Willow Street streetcar barn in the Carrollton neighborhood.

Serenading the crowd are the Storyville Stompers, who join the PPP for the ride. Across Willow Street from the car barn stands a group of about ten people referred to by the Phellows as the Mystery Maskers. Dressed in street clothes but masked, they hold up poster-board signs covered with clever, often satirical comments on the current Carnival season.

The Phellows depart from the car barn at 7:30 p.m. sharp. Stowed away on the streetcar are two enormous king cakes that are passed around by the previous year's royalty—one for the guys, one for the gals.

The Phunny Phorty Phellows ride the St. Charles Avenue streetcar route proclaiming the beginning of the Carnival season.

The Storyville Stompers perform with the Phunny Phorty Phellows during their annual Twelfth Night Streetcar Ride.

The Phunny Phorty Phellows ride past historic Gallier Hall, New Orleans' former city hall, during their annual ride on Twelfth Night.

Members are handed a slice and moments later there's a loud yell announcing that a new royal couple has been chosen. The new Boss and Queen have each received a slice containing "the baby."

A brief annual stop during the almost seven-mile ride takes place in front of Gallier Hall, for many years New Orleans' city hall. Dedicated in 1853, the building, which resembles a Greek temple, is where the Mystery Maskers ask the streetcar conductor to stop so that they may toast the new royalty.

Once the Phellows conclude their ride back to the car barn, they scurry over to the Mid-City Lanes Rock 'n'

This member of the Phellows dresses as an owl, the historic Carnival krewe's mascot.

A member of the Phunny Phorty Phellows pays tribute to artist George Rodrigue's iconic Blue Dog.

Bowl for their coronation ball, with musical accompaniment by local favorite Benny Grunch and the Bunch. Highlighting the evening is the "Group Grovel," when the Phellows line up and take a bow before their new royalty.

Members then seek out each other for a dance and fill up the ten dance slots on a dance card.

Earlier in the evening, in the French Quarter, a group clad in medieval garb follows a young lady in armor on horseback portraying St. Joan of Arc. The Maid of Orleans, who saved France, is honored each year on her birthday by a procession through the city's original neighborhood. King cake is passed out to members and onlookers. Formed in 2009, the group hands out prayer cards, candles, and many handmade throws. The group's mission

St. Joan of Arc is revered on January 6 with a procession of the faithful in medieval costume.

Each year the Krewe de Jeanne d'Arc selects a different young lady to portray the beloved saint.

is to foster French heritage and to venerate St. Joan with events throughout the year.

Around town, in addition to the Twelfth Night Revelers Ball, locals hold king cake parties. Yep, Carnival has begun.

Chapter Three

The Sub-Krewes

It used to be that Mardi Gras was composed of parades put on by krewes who built floats that members rode on while throwing beads. Period. Thanks to a combination of creativity and can-do spirit, the celebration has become more multi-faceted. Here are just a few examples.

The Krewe of Muses has included sub-krewes within their procession. Many are walking clubs—or in the case of the Krewe of the Rolling Elvi, a club that rolls on gas-powered scooters. This krewe even has a sub-group of ladies called the Priscillas.

Women's sub-krewes include the Muff-a-lottas, ladies dressed as drive-in waitresses who entertain crowds with their synchronized dance routines. Other groups include the double entendre-oriented Pussyfooters, Camel Toe Steppers, and Bearded Oysters. The Organ Grinders, with their bare midriffs and harem pants, also dance down the street. On a different plane, the Amelia Earhawts dress up as stewardesses.

The Laissez Boys, a group that rides in formation in motorized easy chairs, appeared on the Carnival scene in 2013. With a nod to the *Star Wars* saga there's the Krewe of Chewbacchus and even a group that pays homage to Princess Leia.

Some parades feel compelled to get bigger and bigger. One krewe takes the opposite direction. 'Tit Rǝx is a procession of mostly elaborate floats made from shoe boxes or other boxes of that size. The local firehouse where krewe members and friends gather in the Marigny neighborhood is referred to for the evening as "Gallier Small," paying homage to historic Gallier Hall, the former city hall where traditional parade krewes often stop for toasts from city officials.

Another walking club that takes to the streets at Carnival—twice—is the Ducks of Dixieland. This krewe, which debuted in 1985, dresses as ducks but has a different theme each year, with such examples as "The Parrots of Penzance" and "Waddle the Yellow Brick Road." They usually lead the Krewe of Tucks parade and then can

This giant clawfoot bathtub float is one of the Krewe of Muses' most popular signature floats.

A giant LED-illuminated ruby slipper serves as a throne for the Honorary Muse of the Krewe of Muses. Writer Julia Reed was honored in 2012.

A Rolling Elvi with the appropriate attitude.

be seen waddling through the Quarter on Mardi Gras afternoon. Most of the time they follow the Society of St. Anne from the Bywater neighborhood into the French Quarter.

One dance group that has even performed in the Macy's Thanksgiving Day Parade is the 610 Stompers. These guys, sporting short sky-blue gym pants and red sweatbands, first came to prominence in 2009, appearing in a parade honoring the memory of the late sports radio announcer Buddy Diliberto.

Named after a section in the Superdome where many members sat for Saints games, the 610 Stompers not only dance in parades but also perform for numerous charity fundraising events outside of the Carnival season. Coming from a variety of professions, they band together to perform, as they call it, "extraordinary moves."

A walking club that calls the French Quarter home is the Krewe of Cork. Founded in 2000, the perennial king is the affable Patrick Van Hoorebeck, who manages a fashionable wine bar. The parade is always two Fridays before Mardi Gras. The krewe stops for lunch and tops off their celebration with a king and queen's party that evening.

For dog lovers, there's the Krewe of Barkus, which parades in the French Quarter on a Sunday afternoon two weeks before Carnival. Beginning in 1993, local bar owner Thomas Wood decided to make his dog Jo Jo Wood queen of her own parade, hence the beginning of Barkus. Following a theme each year, owners costume their dogs and, of course, parade with their pets. There's a king and queen of Barkus each year along with a royal court. Parade registration fees are donated to various animal welfare groups, and right before the parade is a pre-parade "pawty."

The Try-Athletes Trike Gang, founded in 2012, has paraded in the Mystic Krewe of Nyx. While many of its members are bicyclists, in this instance they are riding tricycles.

The Muff-a-lottas dance troupe dress as '50s style drive-in waitresses and appear in numerous New Orleans Mardi Gras parades.

A member of the Pussyfooters Dance Troupe. The group performs at many non-profit fundraisers through the year.

The Pussyfooters Dance Troupe perform in numerous parades during the Mardi Gras season. Their annual Blush Ball raises funds for local charities.

The Amelia Earhawts Dance Troupe, named in honor of the famous aviation pioneer, perform in local Carnival parades.

The Glambeaux, an all-female group, pay homage to the historic flambeaux carriers with their own modern take on the torch-lit devices.

The Laissez Boys roll in such New Orleans Mardi Gras parades as the Krewe of Orpheus. First rolling the streets in 2013, the motorized chairs can move up to five miles an hour.

Artist Jeannie Detweiler puts the finishing touches on her float for the 'tit Rəx Parade, a procession of shoe box floats on wheels.

Confetti adds to the celebration of the annual Krewe of Cork parade.

The Krewe of Cork generates quite a crowd during its annual procession.

Melanie Talia, the 2009 Queen of Cork, hands out beads to the crowd during their annual procession through the French Quarter.

Krewe of Cork member Margarita Bergen wears an appropriate crown of grapes.

From left: 2014 Queen of Cork Amy Borrell, Krewe of Cork King Patrick Von Hoorebeek, and Grand Marshal George Sandeman of the Sandeman family, who has produced port and sherry wines for more than two hundred years. They are passing right in front of St. Louis Cathedral.

Dogs are royalty for a day during the Krewe of Barkus' annual procession.

Members of the Krewe of Barkus follow a French Quarter route each year.

Buster
Ultimate
Grand Supreme
14
years and older
division

This Krewe du Vieux member takes a selfie during the annual procession.

Chapter Four

Leading Up to Carnival

Three Saturdays before Mardi Gras Day, the Krewe du Vieux unofficially kicks off the parade season. It's naughty. It's satirical, with an amalgam of walking groups, many born out of the original Krewe of Clones. Beginning in the Marigny, its primary path is the French Quarter, though it is known to add to its route from time to time.

During the Carnival season, six gay balls are held, all of them open to the public by ticket. Some of them are staged at the Frederick J. Sigur Civic Center in Chalmette in St. Bernard Parish, not far from the Orleans Parish line. Gay ball organizations, which first started in New Orleans in the early 1960s with the Krewe of Yuga, were severely affected by the AIDS epidemic of the 1980s and '90s.

Parades officially kick off two weekends before Mardi Gras. Many krewes, including the Knights of Sparta, with its mule-drawn king's float, utilize flambeaux carriers to illuminate their rolling tableau. Up to three parades a night can be seen on the St. Charles Avenue route in uptown New Orleans. Among them are the satirical Knights of Chaos, Le Krewe d'Etat, and the all-female Krewes of Muses and Nyx. The ladies were joined by the primarily African American Krewe de Femme Fatale in 2015.

On the Saturday before Mardi Gras, Endymion, the largest parade in Carnival with more than three thousand riders, follows a Mid-City neighborhood route, primarily on Canal Street. Their nine-unit "Pontchartrain Beach, Then and Now" float pays homage to the city's beloved amusement park, which closed in 1983. Among the parades on the St. Charles Avenue route earlier that

Mounted units of the New Orleans Police Department help maintain crowd control during the parade season.

day are the Krewes of Tucks and Iris, the oldest women's krewe, which debuted in 1959.

On Sunday evening look for Bacchus, the original super-krewe, with such signature floats as the family of King Kong and an enormous alligator made of fiberglass called "Bacchagator."

On the next day, a highlight is the Krewe of Mid-City parade. Sadly, its route no longer includes the Mid-City neighborhood, but its floats made of tin foil are attractive and novel.

Before 1987, the Monday before Carnival pretty much meant getting ready for the next day and attending the Proteus parade. That was it.

From the 1880s up until 1917, Rex would arrive on Monday by boat on the Mississippi at the foot of Canal Street and travel by carriage to Gallier Hall, where he was to be greeted by the mayor of New Orleans and other city dignitaries.

This lost tradition was brought back to life as Lundi Gras when Errol Laborde, *New Orleans Magazine* editor and Carnival historian, came up with the idea of having Rex return on that Monday, this time to greet his royal subjects, be honored with a brass band, exchange greetings with the mayor and local Consular Corps, and experience a festive fireworks show.

On the mayor of New Orleans' Mardi Gras Task Force at that time, Errol was able to muster support from the city, the Rex Organization, the Coast Guard, and Riverwalk Marketplace (now the Outlet Collection at Riverwalk) to stage the event.

A few years later, the Zulu Organization began arriving nearby on the river and in 1999 asked if they could come and visit Rex at the event and even started staging a music-filled festival, also along the river at nearby Woldenberg Park.

In 2015, Rex decided to arrive by rail car, coincidentally the same mode of transportation nineteenth-century Rex took to arrive on a few occasions.

Meanwhile, as the Lundi Gras ceremonies commence, two parades are following the St. Charles Avenue route, one behind the other. This is a great opportunity to view a parade, Proteus, that started rolling in 1882. He is followed by Orpheus, which first hit the streets in 1993. Proteus, named after a god of the sea, is built on a cotton wagon chassis supported by wooden-spoked wheels. Constructed of papier-mâché in the nineteenth-century style, the floats are adorned with flowers and highly sculpted.

Orpheus is directly inspired by these older Mardi Gras techniques but has created floats of much larger size with a papier-mâché flower count that would rival the Garden of Eden. Named after a god of music, this krewe was founded by theatre director Sonny Borey and the locally born Grammy winner Harry Connick, Jr. While the focus is more on the floats, you can't help but notice the musical celebrities that are very much a part of this rolling tableau.

Orpheus' signature floats are among the most spectacular of the season, including a fire-breathing illuminated dragon known as Leviathan, a Trojan Horse, and a giant replica of the nineteenth-century Smokey Mary train, which once connected passengers from Lake Pontchartrain with the French Quarter.

Time to go home and get ready for the big day!

These Krewe of Satyricon polo players even include a polo pony as part of their costumes during the krewe's annual ball.

This king's float is drawn by mules, a throwback to the way most Mardi Gras floats were transported up until 1950.

This parade lieutenant is in charge of the krewe's flambeaux carriers, who help illuminate many New Orleans Mardi Gras parades.

The Knights of Chaos pokes fun at local and national politics.

Le Krewe d'Etat, known for its satirical take on local topics, features a member known as the Dictator, who rides at the head of the parade.

The Krewe of Nyx, a female krewe, hands out decorated purses as their signature throw.

A masker from Krewe of Muses. Note the wig mop and Mr. Clean bubbles.

These two Muses maskers indicate that their favorite New Orleans Saint wears number nine on his jersey—Drew Brees.

The Krewe of Endymion's "Pontchartrain Beach, Then and Now" is a nine-unit float that is considered the largest in the New Orleans Mardi Gras.

The Krewe of Tucks' king's throne is a giant replica of a toilet. This whimsical krewe parades on the Saturday before Mardi Gras.

One of the most unique parades of the Carnival season is created by the Krewe of Mid-City. Foil is used to decorate each float.

At the annual Lundi Gras celebration on the Mississippi Riverfront, the King of Zulu pays a visit to Rex, the King of Carnival, during a special ceremony that includes a greeting from the mayor of New Orleans and a fireworks display. At left is Errol Laborde, master of ceremonies.

This float shows the nineteenth-century Carnival papier-mâché techniques used by the builders of the Krewe of Hermes parade.

First appearing on the streets of New Orleans in 1882, the Krewe of Proteus constructs its floats in a traditional nineteenth-century style.

The Krewe of Orpheus' smoke-breathing Leviathan, which depicts a mythical sea creature, is illuminated by LED lights that sparkle as it moves down the parade route. Sound effects have also been incorporated into the float. Built by Kern Studios.

Flowers are prominent on the floats of the Krewe of Orpheus. This is an homage to nineteenth-century Mardi Gras float design.

A float recalling the famed Smokey Mary train, a popular local mode of transportation in the late nineteenth century, is seen each year in the Orpheus parade.

Note the ominous message on the apron of the North Side Skull and Bones Gang member.

Chapter Five
The Black Carnival

Since the nineteenth century, children in the Treme neighborhood adjacent to the French Quarter braced themselves early on Mardi Gras morning. Men dressed as skeletons came running down the street, knocking on doors. Spouting a message equivalent to "You better behave or the Boogeyman will come after you," they both entranced and horrified little ones. These men were known as Bone Gangs. By the early 2000s, the tradition had almost disappeared. The late Al Morris, longtime North Side Skull and Bones Gang big chief, was among the last of the old guard. Thankfully musician and former National Park Service Ranger Bruce "Sunpie" Barnes has taken on the leadership. The group has grown and now even has its own Facebook page.

Carrying forth the traditions of costume making from their working-class forbearers, gang members construct papier-mâché heads from newspapers coated in flour mixed with water that cover a wire outline of a skull. The skeleton costumes, which include an apron, are made from inexpensive fabrics. Emblazoned on the apron the gang wears is the group's motto: "You Next."

With a heritage that goes back to when escaped slaves sought safety with local Indians, the Mardi Gras Indians are a treasured part of the New Orleans Carnival. Groups, known as tribes, hand stitch a new costume every year that is intricately adorned with feathers and beads. In the last half of the twentieth century, many of the Indians were longshoremen. The tradition of parading is called "masking Indian." The first tribe was the Creole Wild West.

Leading the tribes are a big chief, a spy boy to scout if other tribes are nearby, and a flag boy. In earlier days, the tribes would fight each other. Today it is more of a competition to see "who's the prettiest," to quote the late Indian Chief Allison "Tootie" Montana, big chief of the Yellow Pocahontas Tribe.

By the early 1970s, alternative weekly papers started covering the Indians. Over the last forty-plus years the New Orleans Jazz and Heritage Festival has provided a showcase for the tribes, offering the public a rare chance to see them performing their songs and chants. Many of the groups come out for their Super Sunday event around St. Joseph's feast day.

In the HBO television series *Treme* (2010-2013), two of the main characters are based on the lives of the late Donald Harrison, Sr., longtime big chief of the Guardians of the Flame tribe, and his son, renowned musician Donald Harrison, Jr., who is a leader in the tribe. There are also female Mardi Gras Indians. Daughter Cherice Harrison-Nelson is the big queen of the tribe.

More than a dozen tribes comprise the Mardi Gras Indian Council, which helps preserve and advance the Mardi Gras Indian traditions. There is also a Mardi Gras Indian Hall of Fame and a new group called the New Orleans Black Indian Alliance.

The Zulu Organization was created as a parody of the white New Orleans Carnival. Making its debut in 1909, a group of laborers organized a club named The Tramps. Members went to see a musical comedy performed by a group called The Smart Set, and in the comedy was a skit

This Mardi Gras Indian pays tribute to the late Larry Bannock, the longtime big chief of the Golden Star Hunters.

concerning the Zulu Tribe called "There Will Never Be a King Like Me." The Tramps adopted the Zulu name. This tiny group has grown into a large organization with a Mardi Gras parade and community involvement throughout the year. In addition to a king and queen, who are chosen through an election, other members hold such titles as "big shot" and "witch doctor." One of the krewe's unique traditions is that all float riders wear blackface.

The Original Illinois Club holds an annual ball that originated in 1895. Tradition has it that the organization's name came from the fact that so many members were Pullman porters on the Illinois Central Railroad. The club enabled the children of the porters an opportunity to be presented to family and friends in a ball setting. A dance called the Chicago Glide is a ball tradition that continues to present day. There is also a ball staged by the Young Men's Illinois Club, which debuted in 1927.

Around 1912, prostitutes from the Black Storyville neighborhood near today's city hall would parade around the neighborhood dressed as baby dolls. Clothed in short satin skirts and wearing bloomers and garters, they would ask men for dollar bills and stick them under their garters.

Through the years the prostitute connection would fade away and other groups of women would dress the same way same on Mardi Gras. Just as the tradition was dying out, there are now some revelers who have embraced the baby doll look. Most recently, choreographer Millisia White started the Baby Doll Ladies dance group.

The Baby Doll traditions have been documented in the book *The "Baby Dolls": Breaking the Race and Gender Barriers of the New Orleans Mardi Gras Tradition* by Kim Marie Vaz.

Note the intricate beadwork and feather design in this Mardi Gras Indian's costume.

In the 2015 Mardi Gras season, a new parade debuted called the Mystic Krewe of Femme Fatale. Members of the women's krewe are primarily African American. Their signature throw is a designer ladies' compact.

The Mardi Gras Indian tradition is shared by many black New Orleans families early on. Most of the tribe members' costumes are made by hand and take a full year to create.

Note the intricate design of this Zulu officer's headdress.

These ladies are portraying Baby Dolls, a dress-up tradition first adopted by prostitutes in the early 1900s but eventually embraced by other members of the local black community.

Chapter Six

Celebrities

It all started in 1968 with entertainer Danny Kaye: a new krewe named Bacchus, after the Roman god of wine. They staged a parade on the Sunday before Mardi Gras. Since some of the key players were members of the hospitality industry, one of the goals was to have another parade to help fill out the weekend, therefore encouraging visitors to stay for a long weekend that would last until Ash Wednesday.

Bacchus doesn't have a king. A celebrity, taking on the role of the god Bacchus, leads the parade. Luminaries have included Bob Hope, Jackie Gleason (word was that he was a bit grumpy, having just started to quit smoking), Charlton Heston, William Shatner, Nicolas Cage, Billy Crystal, Drew Brees, and Will Ferrell, to name a very few.

The Krewe of Endymion (which has a king whose name is drawn from its membership) touts a grand marshal,

Actor Nicolas Cage rode as Bacchus in 2002.

while Orpheus boasts many music stars as a nod to their mythological namesake, who was known to be pretty good strumming his lyre. Grammy winner and New Orleans-born Harry Connick, Jr., is the co-captain of Orpheus and actually served as a Bacchus before he began his own parade. Longtime New Orleans theatre director Sonny Borey is the other co-captain.

Singer Willie Nelson served at Bacchus' grand marshal in 2006.

Elijah Wood, best known as Frodo Baggins in The Lord of the Rings *films, was Bacchus in 2004.*

New Orleans Saints quarterback Drew Brees was Bacchus in 2010.

Hugh Laurie, star of the television series House, reigned as Bacchus in 2014.

Crooner Harry Connick, Jr., who reigned as Bacchus in 1993, started his own parade, Orpheus, which debuted in 1994.

C. C. H. Pounder, one of the stars of CBS's NCIS: New Orleans, rode as a grand marshal in the 2015 Orpheus parade.

Television celebrities Anderson Cooper and Kelly Ripa served as co-grand marshals during the 2014 Endymion parade.

Filmmaker Spike Lee rode as a grand marshal in the 2003 Zulu parade.

Singer Kelly Clarkson was the featured performer at the Krewe of Endymion's 2013 Extravaganza.

Chapter Seven

Children at Carnival

Looking at Mardi Gras home movies from the 1940s and '50s, children are invariably clothed as clowns and cowboys for a day. I've actually seen a 1941 film clip of a Shirley Temple look-alike dressed as Bonnie Blue Butler from the movie *Gone With the Wind*.

These days clowns continue to be spotted among the crowd, but superhero-themed garb seems to be at the top of the popularity ladder.

And speaking of ladders, wooden ladders topped with a small rail-enclosed bench have become increasingly popular. These perches provide little ones with a great view of parades and are fixtures along parade routes, especially St. Charles Avenue.

While today's catch consists of myriad types of items, throws adored by children from the 1940s through the mid-1960s included glass beads from Czechoslovakia, straw finger pulls, and beads made from kernels of rice in a wax-paper bag. And if the kids didn't catch anything, a parent's plan B would be to buy a stuffed animal or plastic Kewpie doll attached to a bamboo cane from a street vendor.

Founded in 1983, the Krewe of Little Rascals is named after the famous group of kids from TV and film. They parade in Metairie, a New Orleans suburb. Members range in age from two to eighteen years old. Today they average more than two hundred members.

Currently, Little Rascals has fourteen to twenty floats each year, including court floats, krewe floats, and a specially designed float for handicapped riders.

Some local schools also stage their own mini-parades that circle their neighborhoods. KIPP McDonogh 15 Primary in the French Quarter is one such school; children wear costumes that they make with the aid of RickRACK, a non-profit that teaches organizational skills and provides a chance for children to be creative with the creation of costumes.

With a bench-topped wooden ladder as their perch, these two princesses have a front-row seat for the parade.

Beginning in the 1920s, the Children's Carnival Club began staging an annual ball where younger folk portray monarchs with a full court, complete with pages. The event includes a tableau consisting of a dance performance.

But for several young boys, the real honor is to be a page at a ball. Pages assist the king and queen with their mantles and follow their monarchs around the dance floor for the ceremonial marches.

For most children, Mardi Gras activity will consist of attending parades. The costumes go back into the closet, but in many New Orleans homes the beads on doorknobs around the house will be around long after Ash Wednesday.

This youngster contemplates his most recent catch.

This young student at the KIPP McDonogh 15 Primary School wears a Mardi Gras gown she has made for the school's parade.

A good day's haul for this young parade goer.

Doubloons were first thrown by riders in the Rex parade in 1960.

Keeping beads untangled is the goal of every float rider.

Chapter Eight

Throw Business

While it's still somewhat inconclusive, the earliest record of a rider throwing items off a Mardi Gras float goes back to 1871, when the Twelfth Night Revelers had a Christmas-themed float and riders threw candy. Esteemed New Orleans author Lyle Saxon, in his book *Fabulous New Orleans,* talks about catching beads in 1913.

By the 1950s, glass beads from Czechoslovakia were popular, eventually giving way to less-expensive Japanese imports called "bugle beads," made out of tubes of glass. Today, China is the primary supplier. Other throws popular in the '50s were straw finger pulls and beads made from rice.

Doubloons were first introduced by Rex in 1960. H. Alvin Sharpe, a local artist, came up with the idea and pitched it to Darwin Fenner, then captain of the Rex Organization. While doubloons continue to be sought after, they are being quickly scooped by plastic cups and themed beads. The size of beads have also increased, warranting yet another reason why it is best to not stand too close to a float.

The Krewe of Muses gets a kick out of conveying their signature shoe theme by not only handing out decorated shoes but also throwing beads with tiny red (ruby?) slippers attached to them. Every year the krewe tries to top itself with the variety of trinkets it throws, including bracelets of tiny shoes, cell phone cases, small paper tablets, and plush items.

The Krewe of Nyx hands out decorated purses. Beads that become illuminated at the flip of a switch or by poke are growing popular. Le Krewe d'Etat showers crowds with a wide selection of blinking items, including skull pendants. There's even a tote bag folded up in a banana-shaped fabric carrier.

Of course, one of the most-prized items to receive is a decorated coconut, given out by the Krewe of Zulu. Members of the organization are encouraged to decorate the coconuts themselves.

Beads of all varieties are thrown during the Mardi Gras season.

As this member of Pete Fountain's Half-Fast Walking Club will attest, these days beads come in many sizes.

Beads continue to be a popular throw in the New Orleans Carnival.

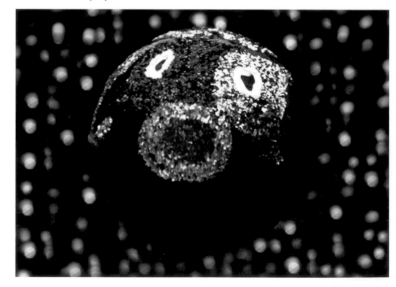

The most sought after signature throw in Mardi Gras is a Zulu coconut.

This Zulu officer favors a New Orleans Saints-themed decorated coconut.

After a parade, it's inevitable that some beads end up in the streets.

Flag teams that accompany marching bands are a common sight in New Orleans Carnival parades.

Chapter Nine

Let There Be Music

While it's so easy to get distracted by the sights of Mardi Gras, it's the sounds that make the season all the richer. It can't be helped. There are actual city regulations that require a certain number of bands to be in a Mardi Gras parade. And, of course, a parade without music is hardly worth standing on the curb for.

Many of the Mardi Gras parade bands are from local high schools. The St. Augustine High School "Marching 100" is always a highlight. Dressed in their dapper deep-purple uniforms, this band has not only played for parades but for Super Bowls, presidential inaugurations, and even a pope.

New Orleans brass bands in parades are fewer in number these days, but the Krewe du Vieux, a small satirical pageant, has consistently featured this kind of music.

Some of the krewes include bands on floats or trucks. Performing in a few parades on a specially outfitted black school bus is the popular Yat Pack band.

The Marine Corps Band New Orleans plays in several parades and at balls during the season. The group's activities is capped off by their performance at the Rex Organization's annual ball, streamed live and televised on WYES-TV.

What's a nice accompaniment to the season are Carnival–connected tunes that can be heard on local radio each year. Many were written during the golden age of New Orleans rhythm and blues.

The late pianist/ singer Henry Roeland "Roy" Byrd, better known as "Professor Longhair," recorded his most popular version of "Go to the Mardi Gras" in 1959. Al Johnson's bouncy "Carnival Time" was recorded in 1960. He's still performing and, after many years, secured full rights to his beloved composition. In 1964, together with composer Earl King, Longhair scored again in the Mardi Gras music pantheon with the tune "Big Chief."

This member of the Warren Easton High School Color Guard is also a proud senior.

The St. Augustine High School Band comprises one hundred musicians and is one of the most popular marching bands in Carnival.

The Mardi Gras Indian tribe Wild Magnolias left their own mark on the season with "Handa Wanda" in 1970.

It's hard to choose a favorite Mardi Gras season song, but upon hearing the first few seconds of Professor Longhair's whistling on "Go to the Mardi Gras" it is possible for the heart of a Carnival lover to skip a beat.

The Southern University Marching Band, which is known as the Human Jukebox because of its vast repertoire, has 230 members.

This tiny drum major still means business.

Members of Cork Poppas Brass Band play in the walking Krewe of Cork's annual parade in the French Quarter.

Members of the Marine Corps Band New Orleans march in numerous Mardi Gras parades.

This bagpipe player shows the variety of music that can be seen in a Mardi Gras parade.

With more than fifty Mardi Gras parades in the area, New Orleans children are exposed to many music instruments at an early age.

Singer Al Johnson's "Carnival Time" has become one of Mardi Gras' most beloved songs.

A Zulu officer stands atop his float on Canal Street.

Chapter Ten

Mardi Gras Day

Waiting for Zulu and Rex under the oaks of St. Charles Avenue with the smell of grilling hot dogs pervading the air. Meandering through the French Quarter in search of over-the-top costumes and occasionally spotting someone with a little—or maybe no—top. Following the path of the Mardi Gras Indians to the corner of N. Claiborne and Orleans Avenues. Carnival day is given structure with parades. But within those twenty-four hours are limitless possibilities.

Folks who choose uptown get to see first glimpses of Zulu and Rex as they proceed downtown to Canal Street adjacent to the French Quarter. The Caribbean-themed Krewe of Mondo Kayo walking club also meanders down the avenue.

In the Quarter, Bourbon Street begins to swell with people, and the interplay of revelers throwing beads from balconies to folks down on the street begins in full force. This is the street where the upper torso is sometimes bared for beads and is also the site of an elaborate gay costume contest.

Elsewhere, Mardi Gras Indian tribes gather to strut their stuff. The gatherings are more peaceful than in the olden days when fights would break out between tribes.

In the last decade the tradition of some black Orleanians dressing as skeletons has been revived. And also experiencing a somewhat modified comeback are the Baby Dolls. Originally black prostitutes who dressed as baby dolls on Mardi Gras day, today the dress-up custom has been adopted mostly by black ladies who aren't "of the evening" and just enjoy having a good time.

Meanwhile, in the Bywater neighborhood outside the French Quarter, folks are donning their costumes, many of them elaborate, to meet up at a home for breakfast before the journey on foot. During that journey they will be serenaded by the Storyville Stompers Brass Band through Bywater, Marigny (with a stop to "fortify" themselves), and into the Quarter to end at Canal Street, hopefully in time to view Rex.

Sometimes group members pay a visit to the Moon Walk near Café du Monde. This public promenade along the Mississippi is the place the group has chosen to sprinkle the ashes of members who have died the previous year upon the water of the river.

With a building lined with photos from more than a century's worth of parading, the Jefferson City Buzzards take to the streets during the Carnival season twice. They first started parading in 1890. Two weeks before Mardi Gras they have a "practice parade." Dressed in drag, they stop at neighborhood watering holes for a drink or two.

Their circuitous Mardi Gras morning route begins on the edge of Audubon Park, near Magazine Street. They eventually hit St. Charles Avenue and precede Rex. They also parade in Metairie for the St. Patrick's Day parade (which is on the Sunday before March 17) and the annual Irish-Italian parade (the Sunday following).

As for the name, Jefferson City is the historic designation of the area in which the clubhouse is located. On the Mississippi River in that neighborhood was a slaughterhouse. Legend has it that buzzards used to hover around the structure.

The Irish Channel Corner Club isn't too far behind in walking-club seniority. Founded in 1918 on the corner of Third and Rousseau Streets in the Irish Channel, their current clubhouse is on Annunciation Street. In addition to their Mardi Gras day march, they are part of the Krewe of Thoth and the Irish Channel's St. Patrick's Day parade.

The Lyons Club, established in 1946, began at Grit's Bar on Lyons Street in uptown New Orleans. As with the other clubs, the Lyons Club employs bands to accompany their procession. Costumed in satin tops and pants, they, too, march in the Irish Channel St. Patrick's Day parade.

Founded in 1961, revered clarinetist Pete Fountain's Half-Fast Walking Club marches on Mardi Gras day, these days with a mini-streetcar float carrying Pete himself performing with his band. Also along to play is fellow clarinetist Tim Laughlin, who considers Pete his mentor.

Their route includes a meander around some uptown neighborhoods until the group stops at Commander's Palace and from there goes down Washington Avenue to turn onto St. Charles before Zulu.

Over on Canal Street, after Zulu and Rex, come the decorated truck parades Elks Orleanians and Crescent City with a combined total of almost two hundred trucks.

By evening, it's time to relax. The parades are over. Many parade goers miss Comus. This parade, which set the structure for other organized parades in 1857, left the streets in 1991. But, fear not, there is still some Carnival activity left.

Rex and Comus currently stage their balls in hotels on historic Canal Street almost directly opposite from each other. And, even if you aren't a krewe member, you can watch the soirees on WYES-TV (within its broadcast area and statewide through LPB2) or online.

As with most older Carnival balls, these krewes stage their balls to introduce debutantes to New Orleans society. Rex also hosts members of the Marine Corps Band New Orleans for a performance.

A ball highlight that has taken place since 1882 is the meeting of the Courts of Rex and Comus. Rex, his queen, and his court walk from the Sheraton New Orleans Hotel across Canal Street on a red carpet to the Marriott Hotel to pay homage to Comus. Prior to Hurricane Katrina, the

Zulu riders hand out coconuts to the crowd.

Comus and Rex balls were held at the Morris F. X. Municipal Auditorium. Rex would have a short walk to the other side of the facility where the Comus ball was being held. In earlier days, the meeting would entail a carriage ride across town.

After Rex and Comus meet, they and their queens engage in a grand march; there is a bit more general dancing and the curtain comes down on another Carnival.

While the ball concludes around 11:15 p.m., at midnight, on Bourbon Street, the chief of the New Orleans Police Department and members of the force on horseback travel down the street announcing that it's time to clear out. Mardi Gras is officially over.

In keeping with Catholic tradition, on the next day, Ash Wednesday, many of

Each year artistic director Henri Schindler works closely with members of the Rex Organization to come up with a parade that features an all-original theme and employs nineteenth-century float-building traditions. The parade is constructed by Kern Studios.

the faithful go to local churches to have ashes placed on their foreheads. Farewell to the feasting and on to the fasting of Lent.

Since Carnival was born out of Christianity, it is only appropriate to quote Ecclesiastes: "To everything a season." Looking up at an oak tree on St. Charles Avenue in July at a dangling Mardi Gras bead serves as a reminder that in New Orleans the Carnival season is never too far away.

A stereoscopic style view of Rex's Boeuf Gras float.

Inspired by an 1882 invitation to the Rex ball, in 2012 the Rex Organization introduced a Butterfly King float. It was constructed by Jonathan Bertuccelli, whose father, Raul, also an artist, had been long involved with the New Orleans Carnival.

A contestant in the Annual Bourbon Street Awards, a costume contest for the gay community that was founded in 1963 by Arthur Jacobs.

Actress Becky Allen has paraded with the Society of St. Anne for many years.

The Society of St. Anne walking club, founded in 1969, is a group that gathers at a Bywater home on Mardi Gras morning, proceeds through the Marigny neighborhood, up Royal Street through the French Quarter, and ends up at Canal Street, hopefully in time to view the Rex parade. The founders are Henri Schindler, Paul Poche, and Jon Newlin. Note the ribboned hoops on poles that have become the group's trademark. Today Robyn Halvorsen coordinates the group.

Organized in 1890, the Jefferson City Buzzards is the oldest New Orleans walking club.

Pete Fountain and his Half–Fast Walking Club first started marching on Mardi Gras day in 1961.

The Irish Channel Corner Club marches on the Sunday before Mardi Gras with the Thoth Parade.

Late afternoon on Mardi Gras day at the corner of Royal and St. Louis Streets.

The Meeting of the Courts of Rex and the Mistick Krewe of Comus first took place in 1882. New Orleans public television station WYES broadcasts and streams the balls on Mardi Gras night, a fitting grand finale to Carnival. (Photo by Estelle Egan deVerges)

This masker pays tribute to a much-beloved local drug store chain that is no longer in business.

Queen and king for a day.